ROYAL
MUSEUMS
GREENWICH

National Maritime Museum
Souvenir Guide

First published in 2018 by the National Maritime
Museum, Park Row, Greenwich, London SE10 9NF.
This edition published in 2022.

At the heart of the UNESCO World Heritage Site
of Maritime Greenwich are the four world-class
attractions of Royal Museums Greenwich – the
National Maritime Museum, Cutty Sark, the Royal
Observatory, and the Queen's House.

ISBN: 978-0-948065-99-6

Text by Robert Blyth, Senior Curator of World and
Maritime History

A CIP catalogue record for this book is available from
the British Library.

Designed by Louise Turpin
Printed and bound in the UK by L&S Printing

2 3 4 5 6 7 8 9 10

Contents

Welcome to
the National
Maritime Museum!

The National Maritime Museum is the world's largest and most-visited museum of seafaring. Here you can discover epic stories of exploration and endeavour that have shaped our world today. This guide introduces you to the Museum's main galleries and some of its key objects and stories.

Enjoy your visit and be sure to come again.

▲ Royal opening of the National Maritime Museum by King George VI, 1937, with Geoffrey Callendar (far left), Sir James Caird and the first trustees. King George VI was accompanied by his mother Queen Mary, his wife Queen Elizabeth and their daughter Elizabeth, later to become Queen Elizabeth II. C9138-b

A brief history of the National Maritime Museum and its collections

The Museum's opening by George VI on 27 April 1937 was the result of ten years' preparatory work. This began in 1927 when James Caird (1864–1954), a Scottish shipowner and member of the Society for Nautical Research (SNR), bought a collection of maritime prints, drawings and paintings from Arthur Macpherson, a passionate sailor and voracious collector, on the understanding it would become the core of a new 'national naval and nautical museum'. The author Rudyard Kipling, who championed the acquisition of the Macpherson Collection, suggested a more concise name and the National Maritime Museum was born. Caird was advised by Professor Geoffrey Callender of the Royal Naval College. Callender, also prominent in the SNR, became the Museum's first director and served until his death in 1946. Caird paid for converting the principal buildings (previously those of the Royal Hospital School). During the Second World War (1939–45), the collection's main treasures were moved out of London for safekeeping and the buildings were requisitioned by the Admiralty. The Park Row Wing, which housed the 'secret books' of the Admiralty's M Branch, finally came into full Museum use in 1951.

Since then the Museum has continued to grow and develop, modernising its facilities and improving its displays to meet public demand. In 2018, four new galleries were added, increasing permanent display space by 40 per cent and allowing more objects to be seen and further stories to be told. The galleries and displays allow you to discover ships and boats of all shapes and sizes, voyage across the world's oceans, and experience epic adventures of exploration and encounter. After your visit, the sea will never be the same again.

Your visit in 10 objects

These 10 objects – large and small – provide you with an essential introduction to the rich stories woven through the Museum's unrivalled collections.

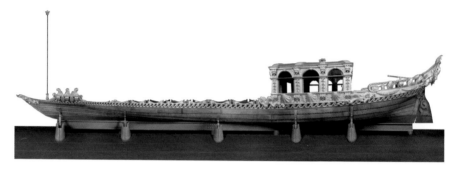

▲ A river limousine: Prince Frederick's barge (*level 0 – The Square*)
Designed and built for George II's eldest son, Frederick, Prince of Wales, this barge was the epitome of luxury and fashionable taste. Frederick, a keen patron of the arts, employed the leading architect William Kent to devise the decorative scheme for the barge. The barge was launched on 8 July 1732 and used that day to take Prince Frederick, Queen Caroline and five princesses from Chelsea to Somerset House. The barge was last used in October 1849 when Prince Albert opened the London Coal Exchange. (BAE0035)

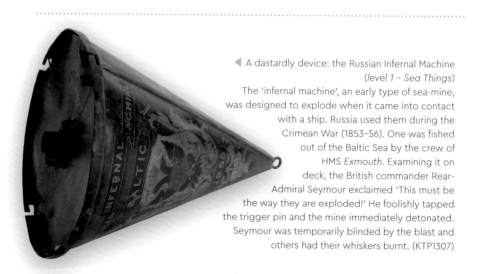

◀ A dastardly device: the Russian Infernal Machine (*level 1 – Sea Things*)
The 'infernal machine', an early type of sea-mine, was designed to explode when it came into contact with a ship. Russia used them during the Crimean War (1853–56). One was fished out of the Baltic Sea by the crew of HMS *Exmouth*. Examining it on deck, the British commander Rear-Admiral Seymour exclaimed 'This must be the way they are exploded!' He foolishly tapped the trigger pin and the mine immediately detonated. Seymour was temporarily blinded by the blast and others had their whiskers burnt. (KTP1307)

▲ Around the world for fun: figurehead
of the steam yacht *Sunbeam*
(*level 0 – The Square*)
Lord and Lady Brassey were the first people
to circumnavigate the globe for fun when
they cruised around the world in their
steam yacht, the *Sunbeam*, in 1876–77.
The figurehead, representing a female
angel, was based on the Brasseys' daughter
Constance Alberta, whose nickname was
'Sunbeam'. On their voyage, they faced
Chinese pirates and endured storms that
nearly swept the Brassey children overboard!
(FHD0106)

▼ A little token of a large ship:
Great Eastern turban shell
(*level 0 – Maritime London*)
When it was launched in 1858, Isambard
Kingdom Brunel's ship the *Great Eastern*
was the largest ever built. Nearly 700 feet
long and weighing almost 19,000 tons, it
was a true monster of the sea. Although a
technical phenomenon, and celebrated in
souvenirs like this engraved shell, the ship
was a commercial disaster as a passenger
liner. However, it found success
laying the transatlantic
telegraph cable.
(OBJ0476)

▶ Small is beautiful: Captain Berry's freedom box
(*level 0 – Voyagers*)
This gold and enamel box was presented to
Captain Edward Berry, in recognition of his
actions as captain of the *Vanguard* at the Battle
of the Nile in 1798. It contains a scroll granting
him the Freedom of the City of London, which
allowed him civic privileges. The lid shows
the most dramatic scene of the battle, the
destruction of the French flagship *L'Orient*.
(PLT0023)

◀ 'My trusty friend': K1 (*level 1 – Pacific Encounters*) The explorer James Cook took the marine timekeeper 'K1' on his second and third voyages to the Pacific in the 1770s. He called the highly accurate chronometer 'my trusty friend' and 'never-failing guide'. It allowed Cook to calculate longitude – his position on an east–west axis. This helped him to pinpoint the location of islands, survey the coasts of Australia and New Zealand, and create detailed charts of the vast Pacific. (ZAA0038)

▼ Humble but heroic: the *James Caird* boat compass (*level 2 – Polar Worlds*) In 1916, Ernest Shackleton and the crew of the exploration ship *Endurance* were trapped off Antarctica in ice that was crushing the vessel. They were forced into boats that were dragged to open water, before sailing to the desolate Elephant Island. With little hope of rescue, a small party, including Shackleton, set off in the best boat, the *James Caird*, to reach help in South Georgia, 800 miles away. What followed was a desperate voyage through treacherous seas using this compass and glimpses of the Sun for navigation. Unbelievably they achieved their goal and everyone was saved. (ZBA1610)

◀ A national icon: Nelson's Trafalgar coat (*level 2 – Nelson, Navy, Nation*) At 1.15 in the afternoon during the Battle of Trafalgar (21 October 1805), a French sharpshooter took aim at Vice-Admiral Horatio Nelson. The shot found its mark, hitting Nelson's left shoulder, passing through his lung and lodging in the base of his spine. He was mortally wounded, but remained alive long enough to learn that Britain had defeated the combined French and Spanish fleet. His uniform coat, bearing the bullet hole, has become an iconic relic of the fallen hero. (UNI0024)

◀ Tudor technology: Humfrey Cole's astronomical compendium (*level 2 – Tudor and Stuart Seafarers*) This multifunctional instrument was made in London in 1569 by Humfrey Cole. It contains a sundial, tables for the latitudes of European cities, calendars, a compass and a theodolite. Although packed with practical navigational tools, this instrument was not designed for use at sea but as a mathematical 'jewel' to demonstrate the owner's knowledge and taste. (AST0172)

▶ Shipbuilder to the King: Jamsetjee Bomanjee (*level 1 – Traders*) The Bombay-based shipbuilder Jamsetjee Bomanjee achieved the distinction of being the first person outside Britain to build ships for the Royal Navy. In 1802 he was commissioned to build a 74-gun teak warship and other orders followed. In his hand are the plans of the *Minden*, launched in 1810, and to the left a ship is on the stocks under construction. The silver ruler tucked into his waistband was a gift from the East India Company for his services. (BHC2803)

Ship Stories

Ships are the essential vehicles of the maritime world. The displays on level 0 introduce the variety of vessels and the extraordinary range of experiences, occupations and equipment associated with a seafaring life, both past and present.

◀ *Discharging Flour*, by John Everett, 1918. PAH6916

Voyagers *(Sammy Ofer Wing)*

The Voyagers gallery introduces the diversity of the maritime world through a range of objects. Arranged by theme, you can discover all sorts of stories. Leisure can be enjoyed with yacht models and seaside souvenirs. Conflict is experienced through swords and guns, including an AK-47, the formidable Kalashnikov assault rifle. The scientific instruments provide an insight into surveying and shipbuilding and grisly medical equipment shows how health at sea was managed. But romance is also present with sailors' love tokens and sentimental ornaments capturing the joy of a partner returning safely from a long voyage at sea.

Watching over the gallery is a large model of HMS *King George V* (1939). This mighty British battleship fought during the Second World War. The intricate details of the model show the vast complexity of the warship, complete with its Supermarine Walrus reconnaissance plane, and demonstrates the extraordinary skills of the model makers.

▼ Contents of naval surgeon's instrument case, about 1850. TOA0132

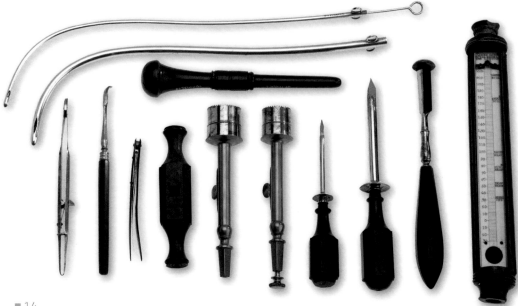

▲ Staffordshire mug modelled as the head of Admiral Sir George Brydges Rodney (1719–92), about 1782. AAA4383

▶ Model of the Royal Yacht *Mary* (1660), scale 1:40, 1949. SLR0369

The Square

You can see some of the National Maritime Museum's largest objects in The Square.

Powering ahead

Miss Britain III, the *Reliant* paddle tug engine and the type-23 frigate propeller all represent different approaches to propulsion. Designed and built by Hubert Scott-Paine in 1933, *Miss Britain III* was the first powerboat to exceed 100 mph in salt water. A powerful aero-engine was used to achieve the necessary speed and a streamlined aluminium body ensured the minimum amount of drag.

▲ Type-23 frigate propeller, made by Stone-Vickers Ltd. ZBA1347

The steam tug *Reliant* (1907) utilised the much older technology of paddlewheels. It was built for use on the Manchester Ship Canal, where it towed larger cargo ships into position, allowing goods to be loaded and unloaded at the quayside. Paddlewheels gave the *Reliant* greater manoeuvrability, which was ideal for Manchester's restricted waterways. The type-23 frigate propeller was not just designed to drive a modern warship through the water, it was also built for stealth. By minimising sound, the propeller helped to conceal the presence of the frigate from any submarines that might be nearby.

◀ The hydroplane hull of *Miss Britain III* (1933). BAE0064

▲ Waterline model of the steam tug *Reliant* (1907), scale: 1:38.4, 1979. SLR0146

Leading the way

Traditionally, a figurehead was believed to help a ship 'see' its way through the waves. Sometimes this 'look' implied danger. The figurehead of HMS *Implacable*, for example, is a representation of Medusa, a mythological Greek Gorgon (monster), whose gaze turned her unsuspecting victims to stone. At least the figurehead of HMS *Bulldog* carries a warning: the animal's collar reads '*Cave canem*'; Latin for 'beware the dog'.

Changing technology, such as the move from sail to steam and from wooden to iron ships, meant figureheads became redundant. But ship badges continue to be a way to give a ship an identity and visualise its name.

▶ A selection of the National Maritime Museum's figurehead collection.

Turner's Battle of Trafalgar
(*The Square*)

In 1822, George IV commissioned J.M.W. Turner, Britain's leading artist, to paint *The Battle of Trafalgar* for display at St James's Palace in London. The finished work, the largest of Turner's paintings, is on a monumental scale (2.61 m x 3.68 m). At its centre, illuminated by sunlight, is Nelson's flagship, the *Victory*, with the battle raging all around in clouds of gun smoke. Turner shows the ship's foremast, shot away by ferocious enemy fire, falling down, considered an allusion to Nelson himself, who was fatally wounded on deck. Flags spelling out his famous signal – 'England expects that every man will do his duty' – fly from the mainmast. To the right, the French ship *Redoutable* has surrendered and is sinking beneath the waves. In the foreground sailors struggle for their lives; some are already dead, others attempt to save those in danger. Symbolically, a loyal sailor holds a Union flag and, adding to an otherworldly sense of mortality, fragments of Nelson's motto – '*Palman qui meruit ferat*' ('Let him who has earned it bear the palm') – can be picked out in the bloodied, translucent sea.

▲ *The Battle of Trafalgar, 21 October 1805*, by J.M.W. Turner, 1822–24. Left: detail. BHC0565

Maritime London *(The Square)*

For centuries, London was Britain's biggest and busiest port. The Thames linked it to the wider world and became a vital artery for the import and export of raw materials and goods. This trade made London wealthy and the capital's wharfs and docks teemed with ships of every shape and size. But London was more than a trading port. It was an important centre of maritime industry from the building of ships to the manufacture of navigational instruments for master mariners.

In contrast to the grit and grime of the commercial river, the Thames was also London's grandest street and a key location for pomp and ceremony, involving gilded barges and smartly uniformed watermen. London remains a major trading centre today, but the working port has moved further down the Thames and beyond to purpose-built facilities like those at Tilbury, the Isle of Grain and Felixstowe.

Building the 'Great Leviathan' (the 'Great Eastern'), by William Parrott, about 1858. BHC3384

Nelson's Ship in a Bottle

Originally commissioned by the Mayor of London for the empty Fourth
Plinth in Trafalgar Square, *Nelson's Ship in a Bottle*, by the British–Nigerian
artist Yinka Shonibare, celebrates multiculturalism and the diversity of British
maritime history. The bottle contains a 1:30 scale replica of Nelson's famous
flagship, the *Victory*. The ship's 37 sails are made of patterned textiles
inspired by Indonesian batik, creating a symbolic 'message in a bottle',
exploring the legacies of British trade and empire that Nelson's
victory at Trafalgar helped to secure. The model was assembled
from inside the bottle, which measures 5 × 2.8 metres,
with the neck just large enough for
someone to climb into.

ZBA9268

Ocean Stories

Oceans cover nearly 70 per cent of the Earth's surface, making it a maritime planet. The displays on level 1 allow you to circumnavigate the globe by voyaging across the Pacific, the Atlantic and the Indian Oceans.

◀ *Blown on the Wind*, by David James, 1898. BHC2311

Pacific Encounters *(East Wing)*

Sackler Gallery

The Pacific Ocean is vast, covering roughly one third of the Earth's surface. The people of the Pacific have long mastered the navigation of this mighty ocean, settling on its many islands and developing sophisticated societies. For Europeans, however, the ocean was unknown until the early 16th century and only gradually explored.

In the 18th century the Pacific became the focus of sustained scientific interest as Europeans sought to chart its coasts and islands, examine and record its flora and fauna, and understand the people and their cultures. At the forefront of this enterprise were the three voyages

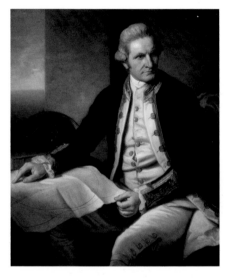

▲ *Captain James Cook, 1728–79, by Nathaniel Dance, 1776. BHC2628*

of exploration (1768–71, 1772–75 and 1776–80) led by James Cook of the Royal Navy. Each voyage was a marvel of navigation and brought back huge quantities of new information that transformed Western understandings of the world. While Cook's aims were commendable, some of his actions on the far side of the globe left difficult and lasting legacies, which still resonate today. Encounters between Europeans and Pacific Islanders were sometimes violent, leading to resentment and mistrust. One such brutal meeting took place in Hawaii on 14 February 1779, when Cook himself was killed amid much bloodshed.

▶ **(top)** *Portrait of a Large Dog (Dingo)*, by George Stubbs, 1772. ZBA5755

▶ **(bottom)** *The Kongouro from New Holland (Kangaroo)*, by George Stubbs, 1772. ZBA5754

In the aftermath of Cook's voyages further exploration took place and waves of European settlers, missionaries and colonial administrators arrived in Australia, New Zealand and across the Pacific. Traditional beliefs and ways of life were threatened and undermined in the process. However, island cultures proved resilient and their revival is a source of pride and a cause for celebration across the ocean and its diverse communities.

◀ *The Head of a Chief of New-Zealand*, by Sydney Parkinson, about 1773. PBC4680

▼ *The War-Boats of the Island of Otaheite [Tahiti]...*, by William Hodges, 1777. BHC2374

Sea Things (*East Wing*)

What is your connection with the sea? The hundreds of objects in Sea Things offer myriad ways for you to find an answer. This gallery delights, tantalises and entertains with its focus on quirky, poignant and unexpected objects. It includes everything from a coat hook made from an albatross beak to a flotilla of ship models, and from busts of naval heroes to ships' bells.

◀ A pocket watch found on the body of Robert Douglas Norman, a passenger who perished in the *Titanic* disaster of 1912. ZBA0004

▶ Lifebelt from the paddle tug *Reliant*. ZBA4718

▶ Staffordshire model of a stout sailor, about 1875. AAA6087

◀ A model Egyptian funerary boat known as the Sacred Boat of Osiris, about 1850 BC. AAE0030

A St Kilda 'mail boat', used to send messages to the Scottish mainland, before 1930. AAB0429

A decorated cathead shield. A cathead is a timber that supports a ship's anchor when it is not in use. EQA0010

A commemorative Barbados penny, made by John Milton, 1788. ZBA2802

Nordenfelt machine gun, 1892. AAA2609

Six-bolt, Admiralty-type diving helmet, made by Siebe Gorman Ltd. ZBA5025

Chair made in 1839–41 from the timbers of the *Royal George*, which sank at Spithead in 1782. AAA3599

Atlantic Worlds (*South Wing*)

Wolfson Gallery

For Europeans, the Atlantic was a huge ocean frontier. It was full of natural resources, like fish, seals and whales, but crossing its stormy waters represented a major challenge for seafarers and navigators. The exploration of the Atlantic from the late 15th century onwards allowed Europe to conquer the Americas, opening up vast new territories for settlement and exploitation, invariably at the expense of Indigenous populations.

In the Caribbean, Britain seized numerous islands and these were quickly developed to grow tropical produce, especially sugar. The backbreaking work of harvesting sugarcane required mass labour and this demand was met by the twin cruelties of the transatlantic slave trade and a system of plantation slavery. For over 300 years, until the middle of the 19th century, more than 12 million Africans were forcibly shipped across the Atlantic in appalling conditions and then sold into a life of slavery. British ships carried some four million Africans, making it the second largest of the trading nations after Portugal.

By the second half of the 18th century powerful forces coalesced to end the transatlantic slave trade and slavery. Principal among these was the unceasing resistance of enslaved Africans themselves, who rose up against the indignities and injustices of their treatment to challenge slavery through direct and indirect action, both violent and peaceful. They were joined by a vocal abolitionist campaign in Britain, which rallied against the inhumanity of the trade and the plantation system. Gradually goals were achieved: Britain abolished its slave trade in 1807 and colonial slavery in 1833. But these milestones were only markers on a very long road to freedom and equality for African people in the Americas.

▲ Bust of Jean-Jacques Dessalines (1758–1806), first Emperor of Haiti. ZBA2482

▶ Cane cutters in Jamaica, about 1880. ZBA2613

Jamaica. W.I.

Cane Cutters.

Traders *(West Wing)*

When Europeans first entered the Indian Ocean by sea at the end of the 15th century, they encountered a bustling trading system characterised by fabulous wealth and sophistication. Rival powers quickly vied to tap into these riches, but England lagged behind. However, in 1600, Elizabeth I granted a royal charter, giving the English East India Company a monopoly on the country's Asian trade via the Cape of Good Hope. This began a 250-year relationship that saw the Company begin tentatively as a spice merchant, bringing pepper by ship from South-East Asia to London.

▶ Chinese vase presented to Lady Emma Hamilton (1765–1815) by the Queen of Naples in 1800. AAA4723

▲ *A trading junk*, Chinese School, 19th century. BHC1182

As it grew, the Company transformed British fashions by importing vast quantities of textiles from India and introducing cotton cloth to the masses. It also extended its trade to China and helped to make tea the nation's favourite drink. But trade also brought conflict and the Company became embroiled in war, conquest and illegal opium as it sought to further its interests. In the early 19th century the British government opened up Asian trade to private individuals and, shorn of its monopoly, the Company ceased trading. However, by this stage it ruled large parts of India. The Company's downfall was swift and brutal. In 1857, rebellion in India caused widespread unrest and appalling bloodshed, leading to the Company's abolition the following year.

The Great Map

At the heart of the Museum is the enormous Great Map, where you can visit every continent and sail through all of the world's seas and oceans.

Baltic Exchange
Memorial Glass *(East Wing)*

These stained glass panels were designed by the artist John Dudley Forsyth for the Baltic Exchange, an important organisation in international maritime commerce, as a memorial to its members who were killed in the First World War. When installed in the Baltic Exchange's London headquarters in 1922, the five principal panels – representing the virtues of Truth, Hope, Fortitude, Justice and Faith – were surmounted by the half-dome with the winged figure of Victory at the centre.

The memorial was badly damaged when the Baltic Exchange headquarters was the target of an IRA bomb in 1992. Following painstaking restoration, it was presented to the Museum in 2005.

ZBA4630

Level 2

Epic Stories

The sea is a place of drama, adventure and danger. The displays on level 2 chart Britain's rise as a maritime power from the Tudor period, through the heyday of Nelson's Navy to the First World War. They also take you to the ends of the Earth with stories of heroism, endurance and tragedy in the polar regions.

◀ *The Destruction of L'Orient at the Battle of the Nile, 1 August 1798,* by George Arnald, 1825–27. BHC0509

Polar Worlds (*East Wing*)

Kristian Gerhard Jebsen Gallery

The polar regions have been a focus for British exploration and scientific enquiry for centuries. The Arctic, and later the Antarctic, became spaces to map and understand, to investigate and discover, to endure and, ultimately, to conquer. They also became theatres of national character and myth, where reputations were made, and heroes sometimes lost.

Early polar expeditions involved searching for the North-West Passage, a sea route around North America connecting the Atlantic and Pacific Oceans. The most infamous of these was led by Sir John Franklin in HMS *Erebus* and *Terror* in the mid-1840s. When no word was heard from the doomed expedition, numerous searches were mounted and it was gradually established that none of Franklin's men had survived. At turn of the 20th century the Antarctic and the challenge of reaching the South Pole gripped the public imagination. Figures like Captain Robert Scott, who led the ill-fated *Terra Nova* Expedition, and Ernest Shackleton, who demonstrated daring leadership during the Imperial Trans-Antarctic Expedition, became national heroes.

Today, as the world's climate changes, the polar regions are once again in the spotlight. It is here the most dramatic shifts are being experienced first and the lessons of polar science may prove vital to the future of the planet.

▼ Stuffed Emperor penguin, caught during Captain Scott's Antarctic Expedition in *Discovery*, 1901–04. AAA4136

◀ *A Party from His Majesty's Ships 'Resolution' & 'Discovery' Shooting Sea-horses...*, by John Webber, 1784. BHC4212

▲ *HMS 'Erebus' in the Ice, 1846*, by François Etienne Musin, 19th century. BHC3325

▶ Photographic print of E.H. Shackleton at the wheel of the *Discovery*, 1901. ALB0346.6

Tudor and Stuart Seafarers

(*East Wing*) Pigott Family Gallery

At the end of the 15th century, Europe embarked on a new age of oceanic voyaging, crossing the Atlantic to reach the Americas and rounding the Cape of Good Hope to enter the Indian Ocean. At this time, England's political and commercial focus was domestic and European in nature. However, as the opportunities presented by the 'new world' and long-distance trade became clear, the nation looked out towards the far horizon. Over the next two centuries, England, later Britain, emerged as a leading maritime power, whose wealth and future prosperity were intimately connected to the sea.

▲ Silver counter commemorating Queen Elizabeth I, about 1613. MEC1631

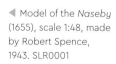

◄ Model of the *Naseby* (1655), scale 1:48, made by Robert Spence, 1943. SLR0001

▲ *The Royal Prince and Other Vessels at the Four Days Battle, 1–4 June 1666,* by Abraham Storck, about 1620. BHC0286

▼ A mariner's astrolabe, thought to be from a ship of the Spanish Armada sunk in 1588. NAV0022

But this was no overnight transformation. England was not predestined for greatness: it had to be worked for and won. Bitter wars were fought against the Spanish and the Dutch. Early attempts to settle and colonise North America proved fraught. The gradual growth of empire was a violent and bloody affair, pitching colonists against Native Americans in increasingly unequal conflicts. Recognisable individuals, such as Francis Drake and Samuel Pepys, rose to prominence in this era. Others less known, like the ordinary seaman Edward Barlow, recorded their experiences for posterity, leaving a vivid account of life at sea in an age of adventure and nation building.

Nelson, Navy, Nation
(South Wing)

For much of the 18th and early 19th century, Britain was at war against European rivals, especially France. The Royal Navy was the country's first line of defence and an institution of considerable national importance. The Navy's ships were the most complex machines of their day and their construction at the Royal Dockyards took place on an industrial scale. The ships were highly organised with crews

▼ *Rear-Admiral Sir Horatio Nelson, 1758–1805*, by Lemuel Francis Abbott, about 1799. BHC2889

▶ *The Fall of Nelson, Battle of Trafalgar, 21 October 1805*, by Denis Dighton, about 1825. BHC0552

rigidly arranged by rank and occupation. Officers occupied the stern of the ship with the captain afforded the greatest amount of space. Ordinary seamen lived on the gun decks. The popular image of the Royal Navy in the age of sail is one of toil, hardship, cruelty and terrible food. While discipline was undoubtedly strict and the work unrelenting, sailors were relatively well fed and prize money (a bounty issued for captured enemy ships) could bring financial rewards, especially for officers.

Within the story of the 18th-century Navy, one name stands out above all others: Horatio Nelson. By the 1790s, he was already recognised as the most talented commander of the age, with his signature 'Nelson touch' of tactical genius able to transform the outcome of a battle. A series of daring victories cemented his reputation. He defeated a major French fleet at the Battle of the Nile in 1798 and prevented the Danish fleet falling into enemy hands at the Battle of Copenhagen in 1801.

▲ A carved inn sign of an ordinary seaman, about 1800. AAB0174

▲ Gold mourning ring commemorating Vice-Admiral Horatio Nelson (1758–1805). JEW0167

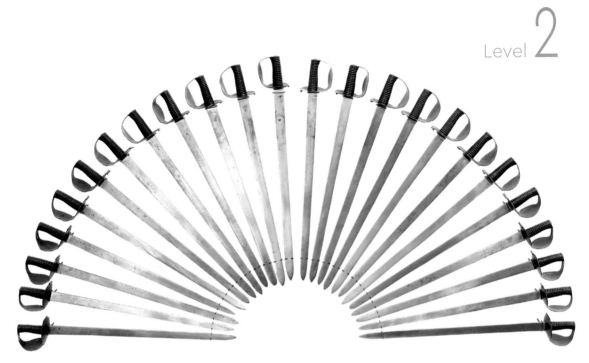

▲ Royal Navy cutlasses, 1804. WPN1629–52

However, it was his final encounter with a combined French and Spanish fleet at Trafalgar in 1805 that guaranteed him iconic status. Although killed in action, he secured a resounding victory. News of his death was met by a national outpouring of grief. Thousands lined the streets of London to witness his solemn state funeral at St Paul's Cathedral, where he was buried with full naval honours. At moments of crisis ever since, the words, deeds and image of Nelson are frequently employed to steady Britain's national resolve.

▶ Horatio Nelson's uniform coat, an iconic relic of the fallen hero. UNI0024

Forgotten Fighters
(West Wing)

The First World War saw conflict and bloodshed on an unprecedented scale. It is, of course, the slaughter on the Western Front that most immediately comes to mind, but the war at sea was a vital element of the ultimate Allied victory. When the conflict began in August 1914, a small number of German warships were scattered around the globe, posing a threat to shipping. The Royal Navy's first task was to neutralise this danger. However, the greatest operation of the war was to secure essential supply lines, bringing materials to Britain and from Britain to the frontline. But, in 1917, shipping losses as a result of German U-boat activity in the North Atlantic became unsustainable. The Navy had to change its approach swiftly, introducing armed convoys and new tactics to counteract the U-boat menace, which could have starved Britain out of the war.

Every imaginable type of vessel found a wartime use, from liners employed as troopships to fishing boats adapted for anti-submarine activities. The Navy proved innovative during the war, playing a pioneering role in the development of air power. While losses at sea were far fewer than those at the front, ships could be vulnerable 'steel trenches'; a well-aimed shell or torpedo could send a vessel and those on board to the seabed in minutes.

▶ Photograph of Katharine Furse, first director of the Women's Royal Naval Service, about 1917–18. A8668-A

◀ Mug made in 1919 to commemorate the end of the First World War. ZBA4394

My Greenwich

(*East Wing*) Mark Pigott Room

The Museum is part of the wider Maritime Greenwich UNESCO World Heritage Site. The 'My Greenwich' space explores the unique history of the 'park-and-palace' complex that forms the historic core of Greenwich.

Henry VIII, Queen Mary and Elizabeth I were all born in Greenwich, which was a much-favoured Tudor residence. It was here that Henry had a permanent tiltyard, where he could indulge his passion for jousting.

The Queen's House – the first neo-classical building in Britain – was designed by Inigo Jones and completed in 1637 for Henrietta Maria, Charles I's queen. It was conceived as a 'house of delight' for royal entertainment. In the 17th and 18th centuries, the Tudor palace was swept away and replaced by the grand buildings of what is now the Old Royal Naval College. These were arranged to maintain the view of the River Thames from the Queen's House.

Greenwich Hospital from the North Bank of the Thames, by Giovanni Antonio Canal, called Canaletto, 1750–52. BHC1827

For Families

There's plenty for families to see and do at the National Maritime Museum! From gallery attractions to toddler groups and weekend workshops, you can keep children of all ages entertained every day of the week. You can visit **The Great Map** (level 1) at the heart of the Museum to discover oceans and continents and plot a voyage across the globe.

Take the little ones to visit our children's galleries **AHOY!** (level 0) and **All Hands** (level 2), where they can stoke a boiler, catch fish and meet pirates! And don't forget to head up to the **Ship Simulator** (level 2) and try your hand at manoeuvring a ship into port.

Family events

There's a whole programme of family-friendly events taking place at the Museum every week. Watch characters leap into existence every Saturday as they lead unique tours of the galleries, explaining about their life and relationship with the sea. Or pick up a trail during your visit and discover objects and stories in the depths of the Museum. The range of trails will allow you to return time and time again, challenging the whole family to explore new galleries and spaces.

Make sure you come back and see us in the school holidays and take part in one of our many planned events. With a range of activities for all ages there's plenty to keep the kids entertained. There are also a number of celebrations taking place each year, including Lunar New Year, Diwali and World Ocean's Day, with music, performance and workshops for the whole family to enjoy. Please see the website for more information on all the activities on offer for families at the Museum.

Research and the Caird Library

The Caird Library and Archive holds an amazing range of resources to help you find out more about the fascinating history of seafaring and Britain's role in world history. Its collections comprise the world's most extensive maritime archive, including unique manuscripts, rare books, charts and maps dating back to the 15th century. These provide extraordinary insights into people's lives and communities both in this country and across the world.

You can register for a reader's ticket online in advance of your visit, which will allow you to pre-order items via our ordering system (rmg.co.uk/aeon). Please bring along some identification when you visit for the first time, in order to be issued with your reader's ticket.

The Caird Library is free to use and you do not need any special qualifications. We have a team of friendly and knowledgeable staff available to help you with your research.

Membership

If you've enjoyed your day at the National Maritime Museum, why not consider becoming a Member? Enjoy unlimited entry to four unique attractions: *Cutty Sark*, the Royal Observatory, National Maritime Museum and the Queen's House all year, including free entry to special exhibitions. Membership also includes invitations to private views, special Members' events, discounts in the shops, cafés and on public events as well as access to a lovely Members' Room and a biannual Members' magazine.

Members may also purchase an annual guest pass at the Admission desk or from the Membership office. There's really no better way to enjoy the adventure.

▶ World map by Francesco Rosselli, 1508. G201:1/53

Support

The valuable support of our Members, Patrons, donors and sponsors allows us to continue our important work – through exhibitions, loans, conferences, publications, learning programmes and community initiatives. Please give generously to help us continue this vital work.

You can donate at donate.rmg.co.uk. Alternatively, you can donate by credit card by calling the Individual Giving team on +(44) 20 8312 6603, or leave a donation next time you visit. Our donation boxes are located in and around the Museum galleries. Every pound makes a difference.

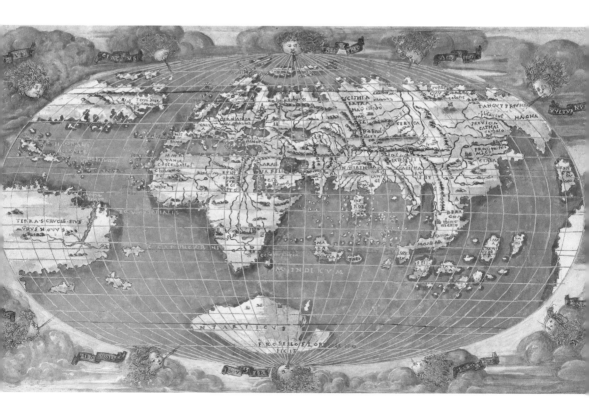

Explore more at
Royal Museums Greenwich

There's plenty more to see and do at Royal Museums Greenwich.
Our Museums are all within easy walking distance of each other,
and together they offer a culture-filled, fun day out for all ages.

Royal Observatory
Home of space and time, the
Greenwich Meridian Line and GMT,
and awe-inspiring astronomy.

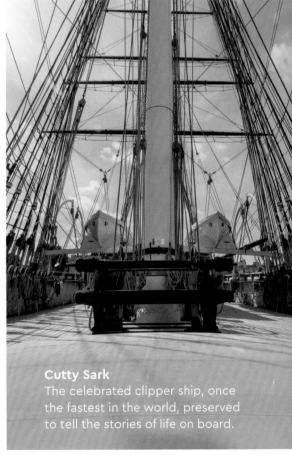

Cutty Sark
The celebrated clipper ship, once
the fastest in the world, preserved
to tell the stories of life on board.

The Queen's House
Inigo Jones's pioneering architectural masterpiece, home to royal history and an internationally renowned art collection.

Peter Harrison Planetarium
Take a tour of the Universe and experience the wonders of the night sky with expert commentary from real astronomers.

Photo credits

2–3, 4–5, 6, 8 (bottom), 9 (all), 10 (top and middle), 11 (bottom), 12–13, 14 (both), 15, 16 (bottom left), 17 (bottom and right), 20–21, 24–25, 28, 29, 30 (top left), 30 (top), 31 (top left and right, middle left, bottom left), 36–37, 38–39, 42 (all), 44 (bottom), 45 (bottom), 48 (left), 50, 51, 54–55, 56, 58–59, 62, 63, front cover **National Maritime Museum, Greenwich, London**

8 (top) **Royal Collection Trust/© His Majesty King Charles III 2022. Photographer: Bruce White**

10 (bottom), 11 (top), 18–19, 26, 40–41, 46, 49 **National Maritime Museum, Greenwich, London, Greenwich Hospital Collection**

16 (top) **National Maritime Museum, Greenwich, London. Presented by the Friends of the National Maritime Museum**

16 (bottom right), 47, 48 (right), 49 (top) **National Maritime Museum, Greenwich, London, Caird Fund**

17 (top left) **National Maritime Museum, Greenwich, London, Royal United Service Institution Collection**

22–23 **© Yinka Shonibare CBE. All Rights Reserved, DACS 2022 / Photo: © National Maritime Museum, Greenwich, London. Commissioned for the Mayor of London's Fourth Plinth Programme. Acquired with the support of The Art Fund; Greater London Authority; Yinka Shonibare CBE; Stephen Friedman Gallery, London; James Cohan**

Gallery, New York; and contributions from individuals, trusts and foundations following a public appeal with The Art Fund. National Maritime Museum, Greenwich, London

27 **National Maritime Museum, Greenwich, London. Acquired with the assistance of the Heritage Lottery Fund; The Eyal and Marilyn Ofer Foundation (formerly known as the Eyal Ofer Family Foundation); The Monument Trust; The Art Fund (with a contribution from the Wolfson Foundation); The Crosthwaite Bequest; The Sackler Trust; Sir Harry Djanogly CBE; The Hartnett Conservation Trust; Sheila Richardson and Anthony Nixon; The Leathersellers' Company; Gapper Charitable Trust; Genevieve Muinzer and others**

30 (bottom left) **National Maritime Museum, Greenwich, London, gift of the Barton family**

30 (bottom right) **National Maritime Museum, Greenwich, London, Fawssett Collection**

31 (middle left), 32, 33 **National Maritime Museum, Greenwich, London, Michael Graham-Stewart Slavery Collection. Acquired with the assistance of the Heritage Lottery Fund**

34 **National Maritime Museum, Greenwich, London, Sutcliffe-Smith Collection**

35, 43 (top), 44 (top), 52–53, 61, back cover **National Maritime Museum, Greenwich, London, Caird Collection**

43 (bottom) **National Maritime Museum, Greenwich, London, Bernard Collection**

45 (top) **National Maritime Museum, Greenwich, London. Acquired with the assistance of The Art Fund**

Stay in touch

 Royal Museums Greenwich

 @RMGreenwich

@royalmuseumsgreenwich

Sign up to our monthly e-newsletter: rmg.co.uk/newsletter